MARY TUDOR
"BLOODY MARY"

By Gretchen Maurer | Illustrated by Peter Malone

goosebottombooks

© **2011 Goosebottom Books LLC**
All rights reserved

Series editor **Shirin Yim Bridges**
Editor **Amy Novesky**
Copy editor **Jennifer Fry**
Editorial assistant **Ann Edwards**
Book design **Jay Mladjenovic**

Typeset in Trajan, Ringbearer, Volkswagen, and Gill Sans
Illustrations rendered in gouache

Manufactured in Singapore

Library of Congress Control Number: 2011924354

ISBN: 978-0-9834256-2-5

First Edition 10 9 8 7 6 5 4 3 2 1

Goosebottom Books LLC
710 Portofino Lane, Foster City, CA 94404

www.goosebottombooks.com

The Thinking Girl's Treasury of Dastardly Dames

CLEOPATRA
"SERPENT OF THE NILE"

AGRIPPINA
"ATROCIOUS AND FEROCIOUS"

MARY TUDOR
"BLOODY MARY"

CATHERINE DE' MEDICI
"THE BLACK QUEEN"

MARIE ANTOINETTE
"MADAME DEFICIT"

CIXI
"THE DRAGON EMPRESS"

To Maya, Kai, and Noa. ~ **Gretchen Maurer**

"Bloody Mary"

Nearly 500 years ago in England, a man stood chained to a wooden stake awaiting his execution. People crowded around to watch. A priest gave the man one last chance to give up his Protestant faith and become Catholic, but he refused—he'd rather die than be forced to worship saints and revere the Pope. Some onlookers murmured prayers, others jeered. The executioner lit bundles of kindling at the man's feet, and soon, smoke stung his eyes. The fire crackled then roared to life. This man was just one of the 284 Protestants that Mary Tudor, the first reigning Queen of England, burned at the stake during her brief reign. No wonder people called her Bloody Mary.

Where she lived

As a young girl, Mary was given her own court at Ludlow Castle.

Mary mourned her mother's death in the seclusion of Hunsdon Castle.

Beaulieu Palace became Mary's own private property on the death of her father, Henry VIII. It is shown on the title page of this book.

Mary was born in Greenwich Palace, on the outskirts of London.

Mary died in St James' Palace, London.

Birmingham

London

Portsmouth

When she lived

This timeline shows when the Dastardly Dames were born.

69 BC	15 AD	1516 AD	1519 AD	1755 AD	1835 AD
Cleopatra	Agrippina	Mary Tudor	Catherine de' Medici	Marie Antoinette	Cixi

HER STORY

Mary Tudor's story began happily. She was born on February 18, 1516, at Greenwich Castle in London. Her father, King Henry VIII, called Mary his "pearl of the world," his "token of hope." Mary was petite, with a pretty face, beautiful complexion, and lovely, long red hair. Henry enjoyed parading her in front of dignitaries in dresses made of gold cloth, flaunting her skills in languages, music, and dance. Mary's mother, Queen Catherine of Aragon, a faithful Catholic, doted on her and most likely taught Mary her letters and prayers. Catherine was the daughter of Queen Isabella and King Ferdinand of Spain, two of the most influential Catholic monarchs of the fifteenth century.

Princess Mary's life was typical for a royal child, until she turned eleven. That's when everything changed. Henry wanted to divorce Mary's mother and marry a woman named Anne Boleyn, who had once been her mother's maid of honor. But that wasn't the worst of it. Anne was a supporter of Protestantism. Protestants, like Catholics, were Christian, but they spoke out against corruption in the Catholic Church. Criticizing the Church for any reason horrified Mary, a faithful Catholic, since Catholicism was the established religion. Henry loved Anne passionately and hoped she'd produce the male heir he so desperately wanted, since Catherine was too old to have more children. Mary must have wondered how her father could do this to her mother—and why he would even *think* of marrying a disloyal Catholic.

Catherine of Aragon, Mary's beloved mother, was the daughter of Isabella and Ferdinand, the "Catholic Monarchs" of Spain.

Mary's father, Henry VIII, was once a staunch Catholic himself, and had even been named by Pope Leo X as a "Defender of the Faith."

Often portrayed as a seductress, Anne Boleyn at first refused the advances of the king, saying "I beseech your highness most earnestly to desist... I would rather lose my life than my honesty."

At that time, as the head of the Catholic Church, the Pope was considered the leader of all European rulers. Divorce was not accepted by the Catholic Church, but Henry asked the Pope to grant him one because he believed, as king, he deserved special consideration. While the Pope stalled for years in making a decision—he ultimately said no—Henry banished Catherine from court and ordered her to live in a remote castle. He wouldn't allow Mary to visit her, thinking they'd plot against him. Mary became depressed and ill, with vomiting, headaches, and pain and swelling in her abdomen.

A painting of the 1529 divorce trial of Catherine of Aragon, by Henry Nelson O'Neil. When the Pope refused to grant Henry VIII a divorce, the king set up his own tribunal.

When Mary was seventeen, she learned her father had divorced her mother and married Anne without the Pope's blessing. Henry's men ordered Mary to hand over her jewels. They told her she'd no longer be called princess or inherit the throne: Henry and Anne's baby girl, Elizabeth, was the new princess and future queen. Shocked and hurt, Mary refused to surrender her jewels unless she received a direct order from the king. She wrote her father several letters, demanding to know if he was serious. He was serious, all right. He'd even locked up a lady in the Tower of London for referring to Mary as Princess Mary, not Lady Mary!

The Tower of London was a prison for high-profile and royal inmates. One day, Mary would imprison her own half-sister, Elizabeth, there.

A while later, Henry's men ordered Mary to leave her family's country manor and move to Elizabeth's house, to help serve the princess. Not only was Mary treated like a servant, but she felt like a prisoner. She wasn't allowed to ride her horse or go for walks without supervision, and sometimes, when people came to visit Princess Elizabeth, she'd even be locked in her room with the windows nailed shut. Mary blamed Anne for everything. She knew Anne hated her. She begged God to protect her father from Anne's evil influence—and to help him remain faithful to Catholicism.

Elizabeth as a young princess. With the tragic history of their mothers and the political rivalry between them, it is no surprise that Mary and Elizabeth were never close. Religion also kept them apart. Mary was a Catholic and Elizabeth a Protestant.

But Mary's prayers went unanswered. Her status did not change, and within the next few years, life got even more dismal. Henry cut ties with the Pope, and Parliament passed a law declaring Henry the Supreme Head of the Church of England, a reformed Catholic church. Mary must have been appalled at this news. The Pope had once named her father Defender of the Faith!

Henry reveled in his new role and soon proved who was boss. To the surprise and disgust of the majority of people in England (Catholics, like Mary), Henry began closing Catholic monasteries. His men sold church land, ransacked jewels from tombs, and burned the bones of saints. Henry pocketed the profit and executed hundreds of people who rebelled against him.

The ruins of many Catholic monasteries and abbeys that were looted and destroyed during King Henry's dissolution of them are still visible across England today.

If Mary felt God was testing her throughout her teens, she must've really thought he was testing her when she turned twenty. Her mother became deathly ill—her father still wouldn't allow Mary to visit—and then her mother died. Mary was so heartbroken, some worried she might die from grief. When Mary asked to see her father a while later, she was further upset to learn she must first sign a document stating that 1) Henry VIII was the Supreme Head of the Church of England and the Pope had no authority in England, and 2) her parents' marriage had been unlawful (she was "illegitimate" with no rights or titles). Mary did not agree with either of these claims. She'd rather "die a thousand times" than go against her mother, her honor, and her faith. She would not sign the document.

One of Henry's men was so angered by Mary's defiance, he told her that if she did not sign the document, he'd smash her head against the wall until it became as soft as a boiled apple. Imagine the horror! Mary feared for her life. She didn't know what to do. Should she sign and betray her beliefs? Or, should she refuse to sign and face death? Mary tossed and turned for several nights. She suffered from toothaches and headaches. A friend urged her to submit to her father to save her life. Finally, with a shaky hand, Mary signed the document. She was devastated. Never again would she surrender her principles.

The people seen in this family portrait are, from left to right, Mary; her half-brother, Prince Edward; her father, King Henry VIII; his third wife, and the prince's mother, Jane Seymour; Mary's half-sister, Elizabeth; and through the door, the court jester, William Sommers.

Mary's father treated her better from that point on. When she moved back to court, he gave her new clothes, a white horse, and a ring inscribed with the words, "Obedience leads to unity." Henry was so pleased by Mary's compliance that ten years later, he even revised the order of succession: Mary became second in line to the throne, after Edward VI, her youngest sibling, and before Elizabeth.

What she ate

Mary dined on meat (lamb, venison, partridge), seafood (carp, pike, oysters), seasonal fruit (cherries, peaches, raspberries, pomegranates, apples), and vegetables (artichokes, leeks, beets, cucumbers). She also enjoyed a variety of cheeses, and her favorite desserts were strawberries with cream and Manus Christi, a candy made from white sugar, rosewater, and powdered pearls, decorated with gold. As a girl, Mary was served up to thirty-five dishes, even though she was considered a fussy eater.

What she played

Before she became queen, Mary didn't just sit around praying all day long. She also enjoyed sewing, hunting, walking, music, dancing, and gambling with cards and dice.

Mary was an excellent musician. She played the virginal, lute, regal, spinet, and harp.

When Henry VIII died, nine-year-old Edward VI, a Protestant, became king. Even though Edward's Protestant councilmen banned the use of rosary beads and altar candles and outlawed traditional Catholic mass and Catholic prayer books, Mary attended mass in private with her staff up to four times a day. When Edward's men found out, they imprisoned several of Mary's servants for almost a year. But this time, even though she again feared for her life, Mary refused to give up what she stood for.

Six years later, Edward VI died from tuberculosis, and Mary was next in line to inherit the throne. Yet Edward's councilmen did not proclaim her queen. To everyone's surprise, they declared Edward's Protestant cousin, Jane Grey, queen. Few rejoiced, not even Protestants. Mary heard the news of Jane's succession and acted swiftly. She met with her household council and ordered her field commanders to prepare for battle. Convinced she was the rightful heir, and acting on what she considered to be God's will, she proclaimed herself queen to her household staff. Her servants cheered, then rallied support.

This painting, painted around 1570 by an unknown artist, celebrates the anti-Catholic policies of King Henry and his son, Edward. The king is on his deathbed, willing the crown to his son, while the Pope is being crushed by "the worde of the Lord"—written in English.

Most people in England were still Catholic. They adored Mary. Within days, hundreds of people donated money and supplies. Thirty thousand men gathered at Mary's castle, ready to fight and die for her. Before long they had transformed themselves into a disciplined army, all lined up in full formation, with military flags flapping overhead. As Mary climbed off her white horse and thanked the men for their love and loyalty, they threw their helmets into the air and shouted, "Long live our good Queen Mary!" Mary was so overcome with gratitude, her eyes filled with tears.

Jane's supporters, realizing they were outnumbered, backed down, and on July 19, 1553, Mary was officially proclaimed queen. Finally, God had answered her prayers. She would bring all the people of England back to the Catholic Church and right her father's wrongs. Londoners went wild with joy—Catholics and Protestants. (Some Protestants believed Mary's miraculous rise was God's way of telling them to give up their faith and become Catholic.) Bells clanged. People whooped and hollered, sang and danced. All night long, they shared food around bonfires, drank from fountains filled with wine, and tossed coins out of windows into the crowded streets.

This 1833 painting by Paul Delaroche shows Jane Grey's execution in the Tower of London. She was only sixteen years old.

Mary's marriage to Philip of Spain, celebrated here both in a painting and a commemorative medal, was extremely unpopular.

But only two months into her reign, Mary learned that rebels planned to overthrow her. They were more upset about Mary's marriage to Philip of Spain, because they feared Spain would come to dominate their country, than her policies of Catholic reform. They only managed to attack Mary's castle with a smattering of arrows before Mary's forces overcame them…and here's where things started to get bloody: Mary ordered about 100 of the rebels to be executed by hanging or beheading. The executioners draped dismembered bodies on gates throughout London. The smell of rotting corpses permeated the city. Mary locked up Elizabeth for a few months, believing she'd been involved in the rebellion, and she ordered Jane Grey to be beheaded, since her councilors feared Jane would always be a threat. Prominent Catholics like the Pope and Mary's father-in-law, the Holy Roman Emperor, Charles V, all supported her policies. But even though Mary's supporters still outnumbered the rebels, this uprising took the shine off Mary's crown.

Still, Mary was more determined than ever to act on her mission to make England Catholic again. For hundreds of years, the Catholic rules and rituals had created order in England. Mary believed Protestants would go directly to hell after they died and remain there forever, and if she failed to stamp out Protestantism, society would fall apart. Friends would turn on friends, neighbors on neighbors. As hard as it is to understand today, Mary believed that by burning Protestants, she was helping the people of England— executing a few, as a warning, to save many.

As soon as she could, Mary directed court officials to lock up influential Protestants, silencing the loudest voices before they could inspire others. They were encouraged to recant (admit they no longer believed in Protestantism), but if they refused, Mary would order their death. Once, however, Mary burned an archbishop at the stake even though he'd recanted: she'd never forgiven him for performing her parents' divorce and marrying her father to Anne Boleyn. Even her advisors did not support this monstrous act.

This picture, from Foxe's Book of Martyrs, shows two Protestant leaders, Bishop Ridley and Father Latimer, being burned at the stake. The color print opposite shows the death of Archbishop Thomas Cranmer.

21

Mary did not witness the executions. She was busy with other matters, like meeting with her councilmen and coping with what she believed to be her first pregnancy. As more and more people were executed, Mary prepared a nursery and sent out birth announcements. But although her belly had expanded and her breasts leaked milk, she wasn't pregnant after all. No one knows whether Mary's false pregnancy was caused by an illness or her desperate wish to produce an heir. She became increasingly pale and wrinkled from anxiety and lack of sleep.

It wasn't long before Mary ordered common Protestants to be executed, too. Most faced death alone, but some were burned in pairs, or even groups. As flames consumed the victims, their eyes bugged out in terror. Some onlookers hollered protests at the executioners, while others heckled the victim or looked on while chomping cherries or other snacks, as if hanging out at a sporting event. But this was no game: the smell of burning flesh would've reminded them of that.

1

2

3

7

What she wore

Contrary to the image of a dowdy Mary Tudor, Mary was once known to be quite a trendsetter. She loved expensive jewelry and gowns made of silk, taffeta, satin, and even gold and silver.

1. French hoods were introduced to England the year before Mary was born by Mary's aunt, also called Mary Tudor, who was at one time the queen of France.

2. Mary inherited her mother's taste for embroidery. Her inner collars were embroidered with Spanish needlework.

3. Mary declared her Catholicism with a cross on her choker of pearls.

4. This huge diamond was a gift from her cousin and father-in-law, the Holy Roman Emperor, Charles V.

5. Mary's husband, Philip II of Spain (Charles V's son), presented Mary with this pearl on their wedding day. After Mary died, the pearl was returned to Spain and worn by different royals for centuries. It became known as La Peregrena—the traveler. Actress Elizabeth Taylor owned it in the late 1960s.

6. Highly valued sable fur was draped over large false sleeves, which were attached to the gown with buttons or ties.

7. Mary often wore a reliquary (a container for sacred relics, like the bones of a saint) hanging from her waist—another sign of her Catholicism.

As far as we know, English women during this time did not wear panties!

Lord receiue my spirit.

The burnings in England lasted for three-and-a-half years. Mary Tudor died at age forty-two on November 17, 1558, some say from the flu, others say from cancer. Just before her death, Mary was spitting up black bile, and she was emaciated and missing many teeth, which was not uncommon in Mary's day. Mary Tudor failed to snuff out Protestantism like she'd hoped, and her Protestant sister, Elizabeth, became queen.

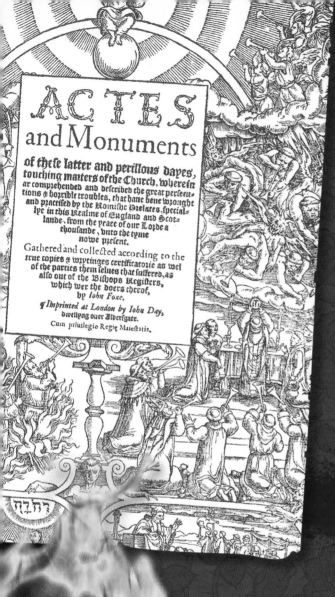

Several years after Mary's death, a Protestant, John Foxe, wrote about the "horrible and bloudy time of Quene Mary" in his book, *Actes and Monuments*. Filled with graphic illustrations of the burnings, Foxe's book portrayed Mary and other Catholic leaders as bloodthirsty villains. With Queen Elizabeth's support, *Actes and Monuments* became nearly as popular as the Bible, and by the 1600s, people began calling Mary Tudor, "Bloody Mary." Today, England is mostly Protestant, due in part to Elizabeth's long and prosperous reign, and some people still consider Mary Tudor—once described as "a good saint…fair as the moon"—to be one of the most evil rulers in history.

GOOD QUEEN MARY?

Mary Tudor was known to her friends and staff to be brave, truthful, and compassionate. One of her admirers even said, "There was never a queen in Christendom of greater goodness than this one." As the first reigning female monarch in England, Mary paved the way for future queens. She strengthened Parliament's role in government, rebuilt Catholic universities and churches, created new trade opportunities, and reorganized the navy. She also oversaw new laws to prevent unemployment, funded hospitals and grammar schools, and gave money to the poor.

Did she deserve to be called "Bloody Mary"? Mary lived in a brutal age. Her entire family had blood on their hands, yet their nicknames are not at all bloody like Mary's:

Mary's grandparents, King Ferdinand and Queen Isabella of Spain, burned to death nearly 2,000 Muslims, Jews, and Protestants. They were called "The Catholic King and Queen" and "The Catholic Monarchs."

Mary's father, King Henry VIII, executed Catholics and Protestants (estimates run as high as 70,000 people), depending on how they displeased him. On one occasion, he ordered three priests to be hanged until they lost consciousness. They were revived just long enough to watch the executioner cut out and burn their intestines. He's known as "Great Harry" and "Bluff King Hal."

Mary's Protestant sister, Queen Elizabeth, ordered more than 200 Catholics to be hanged. After their organs were removed and their bodies were dismembered, their heads and other parts were displayed on city gates. Her nicknames include "Gloriana" and "Good Queen Bess."

© Hatfield House

27

What was all the fuss about?

Sixteenth-century Catholics and Protestants killed each other over their differences—but what were they?

Similarities

Both believed in Jesus Christ and the Bible.

Differences

Sixteenth-century Catholics:

- Relied on rituals and ordained clergymen, like priests, to connect to God.

- Believed that the Pope spoke the word of God.

- Believed that when blessed, the wafer and wine at Holy Communion actually became the body and blood of Christ.

- Only ordained clergymen could lead mass, and they could not marry.

Sixteenth-century Protestants:

- Connected to God directly, without rituals or the assistance of church leaders.

- Did not believe that the Pope spoke the word of God.

- Believed that the wafer and wine at Holy Communion were only symbols of grace.

- Protestant clergy (either lay people or pastors) led worship, and they could marry.

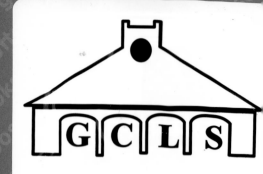